M. C. BISHOP AN

C000148132

ROMAN MILITARY
EQUIPMENT

SHIRE ARCHAEOLOGY

2

Cover photograph
Copper-alloy helmet cheek-piece from South Shields (Tyne and Wear,
England), decorated with a figure of a Dioscurus with his horse.
(Museum of Antiquities, Newcastle upon Tyne;
photograph by M. C. Bishop.)

British Cataloguing in Publication Data
Bishop, M. C.
Roman military equipment.
1. Ancient Roman armies. Military equipment.
I. Title.
II. Coulston, J. C.
623'.0937.
ISBN 0-7478-0005-7.

Published by
SHIRE PUBLICATIONS LTD
Cromwell House, Church Street, Princes Risborough,
Aylesbury, Bucks HP17 9AJ, UK

Series Editor: James Dyer

ISBN 0 7478 0005 7

First published 1989

Printed in Great Britain by C. I. Thomas & Sons (Haverfordwest) Ltd,
Press Buildings, Merlins Bridge, Haverfordwest, Dyfed SA61 1XF.

Contents

List of illustrations

Acknowledgements

We should like to thank a number of people and institutions for their help during the preparation of this book. Lindsay Allason-Jones provided assistance in a number of ways; Peter Connolly lent us photographs from H. Russell Robinson's collection and discussed various matters; Hazel Dodge, Simon James and Lawrence Keppie read draft sections of various chapters — nearly all of their suggestions found their way into the finished text. Martha Andrews also read and commented upon the text, as well as providing invaluable assistance with the final preparation of the manuscript.

A number of institutions kindly permitted the reproduction of photographs: the British Museum (figure 22); Museum für Vor- und Frühgeschichte, Frankfurt am Main (figure 45); Rijks-museum van Oudheden, Leiden (figure 55); Landesmuseum Mainz (figures 16 and 17); the Museum of Antiquities of the University and Society of Antiquaries of Newcastle upon Tyne (cover); Wiesbaden Museum (figures 2 and 3).

All line illustrations are by M. C. Bishop, with the exception of figure 29, 1, which was drawn for us by Anne Gibson Ankers.

Chronology

Republic

338 BC	Latin Wars
264-40	First Punic War
218-02 BC	Second Punic War
149-8 BC	Third Punic War
58-49 BC	Caesar's Gallic Wars
49-5, 43-31 BC	Civil Wars

Empire

27 BC-AD 68	Julio-Claudian dynasty
27 BC-AD 14	Emperor Augustus
AD 43	Invasion of Britain
AD 66-70	Jewish Revolt
AD 69	Civil War
AD 69-96	Flavian dynasty
AD 69-79	Emperor Vespasian
AD 79	Eruption of Vesuvius
AD 79-81	Emperor Titus
AD 98-117	Emperor Trajan
AD 101-2	First Dacian War
AD 105-6	Second Dacian War
AD 117-38	Emperor Hadrian
AD 122	Construction of Hadrian's Wall
AD 132	Bar Kochba Revolt
AD 138-92	Antonine dynasty
AD 161-80	Emperor Marcus Aurelius
AD 166-78	Marcommanic Wars
AD 193-235	Severan dynasty
AD 193-211	Emperor Septimius Severus
AD 253-68	Emperor Gallienus
c. AD 253-7	Siege of Dura-Europos
AD 284-305	Emperor Diocletian
AD 293-305	Tetrarchy
AD 305-11	Emperor Galerius
AD 307-63	Constantinian dynasty
AD 307-37	Emperor Constantine
AD 379-95	Emperor Theodosius I
AD 383-408	Emperor Arcadius

1
Introduction

This book attempts to remedy a misleading impression. Perpetu-
ated and further distorted by Hollywood, the powerful visual
images on Trajan's Column (figure 1) have masked completely
the fascinating evolution of equipment in the six centuries
between the defeat of Hannibal and the fall of Rome.

The approach taken here has deliberately concentrated on
major periods of Roman history, illustrated by a wide variety of
examples. The text could have been divided according to types of
equipment but it is hoped that the present format will prove at
once more useful and more interesting. An attempt has also been
made to say something about the means by which equipment was
produced and supplied to the army throughout the period
covered and it will be evident that this, too, evolved to meet
changing needs.

What is Roman military equipment? The answer is not as
obvious as it may at first seem, for, while arms and armour — the
'hardware' of warfare — are clearly covered by the term, what of
the soldier's personal equipment, his cooking utensils and tools?
There is no simple answer to this, so it is probably easier to say
what, for the purposes of this volume, it is not. Pottery,
jewellery, standards and military decorations are not covered
here, nor are tools dealt with in any great depth.

Arms, armour and related material have much to tell about
Roman society, its technology and its tastes. They can give some
idea of how the soldier perceived himself and was perceived in
society. Moreover, current research suggests that the material
can be used to identify not only particular types of unit but also
different ethnic components within the army. The process of
'barbarisation', which is clearly visible in military equipment and
was long thought to illustrate a decline in Roman standards, was
nothing more than the borrowing of ideas from other cultures.
This went on from the third century BC to the fifth century AD.

The Roman world was never centralised in the way that
modern industrial societies are. It was certainly very bureaucratic
in the later period, but the difficulty of communications over vast
distances made it impossible to run the whole empire from Rome:
it was necessary to delegate at all levels. Nor was the Roman
army uniform (another concept influenced by Trajan's Column).
The archaeological evidence shows that a wide range of types and

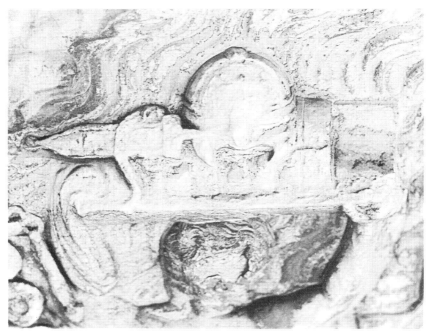

1. Detail of Trajan's Column, Rome, showing a legionary wading, with his *'lorica segmentata'*, helmet, and sword carried on his shield. (Photograph and copyright: J. C. Coulston.)

ages of equipment was in use at any one time. Clearly, the Roman concept of a soldier's 'uniform' was fairly broad; under Roman law he had to keep his weapons and shield with him but uniformity of colour or design was probably unknown.

2
Sources

The study of Roman military equipment is dependent upon three main sources of evidence, each with a distinct, but complementary, contribution to make. However, each also has its shortcomings and it is as necessary to be aware of these as it is to know what they can tell us.

Literary and subliterary

There are basically two types of literary evidence. Direct description is usually found in technical manuals, such as those that deal with ancient artillery, but it also occurs in more literary works where the writer is trying to describe an aspect of the Roman army to an audience that is unfamiliar with it. Description is indirect when a small detail is included in the work of a writer, very often because an unusual feature of the army is dealt with.

It is important to understand that aristocratic Roman audiences, for whom most literature was written, were familiar with their army and did not need to have the practical details explained to them. This helps to explain why the works of the Greek Polybius and the Jew Josephus are so important, for each was describing the Roman army and its equipment as an outsider.

Polybius' *Histories* were written in the second century BC. He was a Greek cavalry commander of noble birth, who had been denounced to the Romans after the defeat of Perseus in 168 BC and taken into the household of the young general Scipio Aemilianus. The two became close friends and Polybius accompanied the general on campaign in Spain and North Africa.

Joseph ben Matthias commanded the Jewish rebels in the city of Jotapata during the Jewish Revolt of AD 66-70. However, he defected to the Roman side and, known as Flavius Josephus and associated with the future Emperor Vespasian and his son Titus, later wrote his history of the revolt. Fiercely pro-Roman, he wrote in Aramaic for Jewish readers; this original was followed by a Greek translation.

The Roman general Arrian describes cavalry 'sports' armour in his *Techne Taktika* and illustrates the use of different weapons in battle in the *Ektaxis*. The late fourth-century or early fifth-century writer Vegetius also describes various weapons and provides some information about military equipment. Even legal works, such as the *Digest* and *Codex Theodosianus*, can be of help. The *Notitia Dignitatum*, a list of military dispositions in the late empire, provides valuable information about the production of equipment at this period and the manuscript preserves some illustrations, although the value of these is debatable.

Both Polybius and Josephus provide descriptions of the army of their day and include details of military equipment. Their accounts are supplemented by material from what can be termed indirect sources. Caesar never bothers to describe the equipment of his troops, since he assumes his readers already know such details, but he does describe unusual events, for example the occasion when his troops did not have time to take their shield covers off before going into battle, or to affix the crests on their helmets (*Gallic War* II, 21). Thus, when he relates how his legionaries' *pila* (javelins) pierced several shields at once, pinning them together, bent and could not be removed (I, 25), it would be unwise to suggest that this was an everyday occurrence in combat. Such snippets of information occur in historians like Tacitus, Cassius Dio, Ammianus Marcellinus and Zosimus, while other writers can be equally enlightening. The elder Pliny tells (*Natural History* XXXIII, 153) how soldiers of his time wore silvered belt-plates and other equipment.

Subliterary evidence is the term used to describe documents preserved on papyri or wooden writing tablets. Papyri bearing both official records and personal letters can be of use in the study of military equipment. A papyrus from Egypt records the organisation of equipment production in a legionary workshop, while writing tablets from Vindolanda (Chesterholm, North-umberland, England) include fragmentary references. Letters home from soldiers on duty in Egypt mention items of equip-ment, with Claudius Terentianus asking his father to send him a sword, pickaxe, grappling iron and two spears, as well as some clothes. At the end of the third century, Paniskos wrote to his wife requesting her to send his arms, armour and tent fittings to him.

Representational
Stone sculpture is the most commonly surviving medium in which the Romans depicted soldiers and military equipment. It may be considered in four main classes: reliefs on propaganda monuments; funerary reliefs; miscellaneous sculptures; and statuary.

In the Republican period, monuments in Rome (figure 6) and Delphi (Greece) depicted soldiers in ceremonial and battle

2. (Left) Tombstone of a first-century AD auxiliary infantryman, Licaius. (Wiesbaden Museum. Photograph: M. C. Bishop.)

3. (Right) Detail of the tombstone of Licaius, showing belts and 'apron'. (Wiesbaden Museum. Photograph: M. C. Bishop.)

situations. Monumental sculpture in the imperial period is represented by Julio-Claudian arches in southern France and examples from the first and second centuries AD in Rome showing 'historical' battle scenes and unarmoured troops. Two columns in Rome, with spiral reliefs running up their shafts, depict the Danubian wars of Trajan (figure 1) and Marcus Aurelius respectively and include thousands of human figures. Trajanic conflicts are also represented on the trophy monument at Adamklissi (Romania). Arches with military reliefs were erected in Rome, Salonica (Greece) and Iznik (Turkey) by late third-century and early fourth-century emperors. Theodosius I and Arcadius completed spiral relief columns, fragments of which survive, at Istanbul in AD 386 and 408 respectively.

Reliefs on Republican-period tombstones (*stelae*) are limited to a few officers in Italy (figure 6, 2). However, there is a large number of first-century AD *stelae*, concentrated mainly in Italy, Germany and Britain, which fall into three types: standing soldiers of all ranks (figure 2); cavalrymen riding down enemies; and groom and horse panels on funerary banquet stones. The practice of erecting figural *stelae* declined in the second century (figure 29, 1) but was revived over the whole empire in the third, with particular concentrations in the Danubian provinces and Rome (figure 40). The fourth century saw a final reduction in numbers with only a few military representations, often crudely executed (figure 54). Reliefs on second-century to fourth-century sarcophagi, mainly in Rome, are closely linked with developments in styles of propaganda sculpture.

Works representing armed deities may include contemporary military equipment, and representations of captured Roman and barbarian arms and armour sometimes incorporate realistic features. Statues of generals and emperors were a very traditional art form and are of little help until the third century AD, when new forms of swords and belt fittings were depicted.

To be of any value in the study of military equipment, representations on stone must be fully understood: the conventions employed, the sculptors' sources of information, the artistic influences at work, the intended function of the reliefs concerned, and the type and quality of stone used. Thus, monumental sculpture in Rome, for example, was often subject to hellenising influences and was based mainly on information available in the capital. It was carried out by skilled artists in high-quality marble that could take a great degree of detail, but it was designed primarily to convey propaganda messages to the public rather than to provide minutely accurate pictures of contemporary soldiers and their equipment. Funerary reliefs in the frontier zones of the empire were carved for military patrons by sculptors who were, perhaps, veterans themselves. Thus, small details of equipment may be closely comparable with surviving artefacts (compare figure 3 with figure 23, 8 and 16), yet elements of stylisation and shorthand conventions must be borne in mind, precisely because the subjects were so familiar to sculptor and customer. The Adamklissi reliefs are most closely related to provincial funerary works because they were probably executed by serving soldiers not governed by metropolitan influences. They are, therefore, a valuable foil to the contemporary Trajan's Column. However, the quality of the stone and the crudeness of style introduce problems of interpretation peculiar to Adamklissi.

Reliefs of deities and statuary belong to very formalised genres and are useful only when they depart from the conventional depiction of attributes. It must also be remembered that most, if not all, Roman sculpture was painted to elucidate the subject matter and this colour is now largely lost.

Representations in other media may be consulted, particularly for the third to fifth centuries AD, when stone sculpture becomes increasingly rare. Frescoes from Dura-Europos (Syria) and Luxor (Egypt), along with Syrian and North African mosaics, provide naturalistically coloured details of clothing. Small-scale representations of soldiers appear as graffiti scratched on plaster (figure 43), pipe-clay figurines, carved wooden figures, reliefs on decorated items of military equipment (figure 29, 2) and metal figurines. Illustrated manuscripts, for example the *Notitia Dignitatum*, are also of some use. However, these diminutive depictions are very weak sources which, at best, usually provide cumulative and corroborative, rather than independently reliable, information.

Archaeological

In the nineteenth century Henry Durden collected a large amount of Roman military equipment by walking over the site of the Roman fort at Hod Hill in Dorset, England. During the twentieth century Sir Ian Richmond excavated this same fort and found more equipment, but this time something could be said about the date and context of the material. Military equipment is commonly found in the excavation of Roman military bases and some sites, such as the legionary fortress at Vindonissa (Windisch, Switzerland), have produced vast amounts. Virtually all equipment recovered in this fashion from the archaeological record is in some way damaged. It is usually quite easy to distinguish damage that has occurred before an item is buried from that which occurs through disturbance afterwards or from the process of excavation. Such material was retained for its scrap value and known episodes in Roman frontier history help to date these finds. The invasion of Britain is one useful dating criterion but known changes of garrison, such as the succession of legions at Vindonissa, are useful, particularly in the case just cited, where each legion's scrapped equipment was dumped on a different part of the same large rubbish heap.

The distribution of military equipment found around the Roman Empire to some extent reflects the amount (and, alas, the quality) of archaeological investigation. Thus, the majority of material now known comes from the provinces of Britain and the two Germanies, demonstrating the diligence of British, Dutch, German and Swiss archaeologists. Less is known from the Danubian region and North Africa and, with the notable exception of Dura-Europos, virtually nothing from the East. This imbalance is now being redressed and material is being published from Eastern Europe which, it is hoped, will make possible a reconsideration of our knowledge of Roman military equipment.

Individual finds of equipment on Roman military sites are usually concentrated around barrack blocks and seldom occur around the administrative buildings. Unusual circumstances can be more informative: the eruption of Vesuvius in AD 79 killed many people and recent excavations on the sea front at Herculaneum uncovered the remains of what was probably a Roman marine, who was equipped with two decorated belts, a sword and a studded 'apron'; in addition he was carrying a bag of tools. The Persian siege of Dura-Europos (*c*. AD 253-7), a Syrian city with a Roman garrison, led to the collapse of a tower where military equipment — including the famous rectangular shield (figure 46) and horse armour (figure 42) — was being stored. A Persian mine under the wall was the scene of a battle between the attackers and the defending Romans, and equipment belonging to both sides was sealed in by the destruction of the mine. Unfortunately finds such as those from Herculaneum and Dura-Europos are very rare.

A high proportion of helmets from the early imperial period has come from major European rivers, particularly the Rhine and Danube. These usually survive in more or less one piece, unlike excavated helmets, which are usually fragmentary. Along with these, many decorated dagger and sword sheaths also come from rivers: this phenomenon may well be related to prehistoric river deposits. Making votive offerings in return for favours from the gods was common practice in the ancient world. The dangerous life of a soldier, combined with such beliefs, may have been responsible for these precious items of equipment ending up in the water.

Some objects were probably taken as booty by the enemies of Rome. The hoard of cavalry equipment from the Rhine at Doorwerth (Netherlands) may have been looted from Roman forts during the revolt of Civilis in AD 69. Although made only of copper alloy, most of these items were covered with silver foil and thus looked very attractive. Large quantities of third-century and fourth-century equipment entered Free Germany as booty, gifts, payment or as items of trade. Ritual deposition in Danish bogs has even preserved some Roman leatherwork (figure 39, 7).

Some military equipment was interred with its owners when they died. This was not normal practice with legionaries or even with most auxiliaries, but it did occur. Such burials are known from the first century AD at Camelon, near Falkirk (Scotland), and Mehrum (West Germany) and suggest that the troops were recent recruits to the Roman army, since their equipment, although apparently native in origin, shows strong Roman influences in its design. Many waist-belt fittings of the fourth and fifth centuries AD come from inhumation burials and can illustrate the way in which the belt was worn.

Experimental archaeology makes an important contribution to the understanding of Roman military equipment. It is in this way that an interpretation of the Roman saddle has been realised and tested (figure 25). Only by building items such as cuirasses or shields can practical considerations such as weight, freedom of movement or weaknesses be assessed. However, the results from such experiments are valid only in so far as they show one possible interpretation that would work: they cannot show conclusively the way in which something was done. The frequent use of reconstructed military equipment for displays by the Ermine Street Guard and other groups and the experience gained by its manufacture are valuable to students of arms and armour, as are experiments such as the march across the Alps in full kit by Marcus Junkelmann and his companions, the results of which were rapidly and fully published.

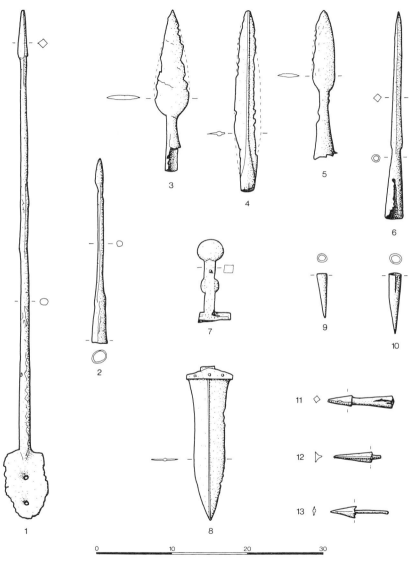

4. Republican weapons: *pila* from Renieblas (Spain) camp III (1, 2); spearheads from Renieblas camp V (3), Cáceres el Viejo (Spain) (4-5), Renieblas camp III (6); daggers from Cáceres el Viejo (7), Castillejo (Spain) (8); spear butts from Renieblas camp III (9-10); catapult bolt from Renieblas camp III (11); arrowheads from Camps of Scipio, Numantia (Spain) (12-13). Scale in centimetres.

3
Republican

The evolution of Rome from a small Italian city-state to a major Mediterranean power was accompanied by a constant process of development in the equipment of its army. The first army was probably equipped in the Greek hoplite manner, a direct result of the Etruscans' indebtedness to Greece. Livy tells how, in the fourth century BC, during the Latin Wars, the Roman infantry began to use the oblong shield (*scutum*) in place of the round one. The Second Punic War (218-202 BC) led to many new types of weapons being adopted from both allies and enemies, and it was this modernised, militarily experienced army that Polybius described for his Greek readers.

The Roman legion was composed of a number of different types of troops, armed in a variety of ways. The *velites* were lightly armed with a sword, a spear and a small shield. The *hastati*, *principes* and *triarii* formed the main body of the legion. Most were equipped with a large oblong shield, a Spanish sword (*gladius Hispaniensis*), two *pila*, a small breastplate (*pectorale*), a plumed bronze helmet and greaves. Men who could afford it wore a mail coat instead of the small breastplate, while the *triarii* fought with thrusting spears (*hastae*) in place of *pila*. There were also three hundred *equites* or citizen cavalry, armed, as Polybius informs us, after the Greek model. They had a stout spear with a spike at the butt end, a 'Greek' shield and a breastplate.

By the end of the second century BC the distinction between the three types of legionary had disappeared and for the rest of the Republican period the legionary was armed more or less like the *hastati*, except that mail shirts were usually worn (figure 6, 1).

Compared with later periods, few pieces of military equipment survive from the Republican army. What little there is mainly derives from Spain, particularly from the fortress at Cáceres el Viejo and from the Roman siege fortifications around the city of Numantia. However, some material from the late Republic was found during the excavations for Napoleon III of the Roman circumvallation of Alesia (Alise Ste Reine, France).

Weapons

The *pilum* was a heavy javelin designed to bend upon impact so that it could not be thrown back by the enemy (although it was a simple matter to repair it after a battle). Livy does not mention the *pilum* in the fourth-century BC army and there is some debate as to whether it was Spanish or Etruscan in origin. However, this weapon is probably depicted on a fourth-century BC Etruscan wall painting from the Giglioli tomb at Tarquinia (Italy). Two types were used in the second century BC, the heavy and the light. The former had a tang and was riveted to the wooden shaft (figure 4, 1), while the latter was socketed (figure 4, 2). Both had pyramidal heads on thin iron shafts, which, it is usually thought, were deliberately left untempered so they would bend when necessary. Similar forms were found at Alesia. A variety of spear-heads and butts has been found on Spanish sites (figure 4, 3-6 and 9-10). No definite Roman examples of the *gladius* survive from this period but its Spanish predecessor was reputedly made of very fine steel. The new form of dagger (*pugio*), which Polybius does not mention, is found in Spain (figure 4, 7-8) and one example was discovered at Alesia. Both barbed and three-bladed arrowheads were found at Numantia (figure 4, 12-13), as was sling-shot. Some lead sling-shot, such as that found at the site of the siege of Perusia (Perugia, Italy; 41 BC), was inscribed with political slogans and insults. Artillery, in the form of catapults of varying sizes, was adopted from Hellenistic Greek armies, where they were first developed. Both bolt-heads (figure 4, 11) and stone shot (figure 5) are known in Republican contexts.

5. Republican stone catapult shot, Camps of Scipio, Numantia. (From Schulten, 1929.)

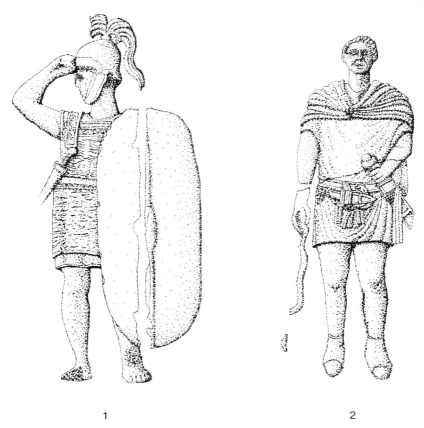

1   2

6. (Left) Legionary from the altar of Domitius Ahenobarbus, Rome. (Right) Tombstone in Padua (Italy) of a centurion from *legio Martia*, dating from before 42 BC.

Armour

The large oblong shield is shown on Republican sculpture (figure 6) and an example (128 by 63.5 cm) was excavated at Kasr el-Harit in the Fayum area of Egypt (figure 7). Polybius tells how the oblong shield was made from glued layers of wood covered in canvas and calf hide; the Fayum shield resembles this description quite closely. It comprises three layers of wood, each made of strips 6-10 cm wide and laid at 90 degrees to the next layer (the inner and outer faces being horizontal, the central layer vertical). This was then covered with a layer of felt and a long *spina* and

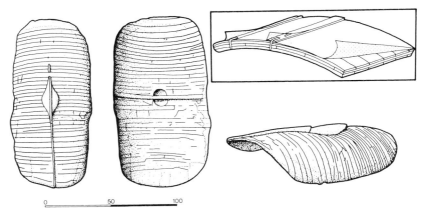

7. Republican shield from Kasr el-Harit (Egypt). Inset shows construction detail. Scale in centimetres.

wooden boss were attached. A reconstruction of this shield by
Peter Connolly weights 10 kg.

Very little Republican armour survives. There is what is
probably a *pectorale* from Numantia but it is circular (figure 8),
not square like that described by Polybius. Some fragments of
what may be bronze mail (*lorica hamata*) were found in one of the
Roman camps at Renieblas, near Numantia. Mail was a Celtic
invention which the Romans adopted. A suit of scale armour
(*lorica squamata*) is said to come from Lake Trasimene (Lago di
Perugia, Italy) but its authenticity has been doubted.

The most common finds of the period are helmets, although
most do not come from Roman military contexts. The Montefortino type of helmet (figure 9), which had its origins in Celtic forms
and dated back to the fourth century BC, was to prove one of the
most enduring pieces of Roman equipment. Although it retained
its hemispherical bowl over the years, the neckguard increased in
size as the type developed. Some examples had crest knobs for
twist-on plumes or crests. The helmet was made of bronze beaten
to shape and was very carefully finished.

Personal equipment

A few belt-plates are known from the Spanish sites and there
appears to be a number of varieties (figure 10). The excavations
at Numantia produced large numbers of both bronze and iron
brooches, essential for fastening soldiers' cloaks. No examples of
Republican footwear or tents have survived.

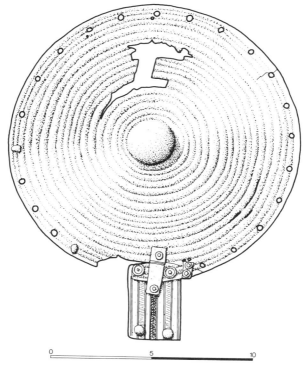

8. Copper-alloy *pectorale* from the Camps of Scipio, Numantia. Scale in centimetres.

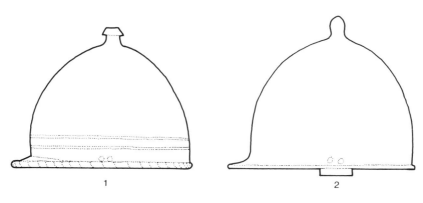

9. Republican Montefortino-type helmets: (left) origin unknown; (right) Castellani (Italy). Not to scale.

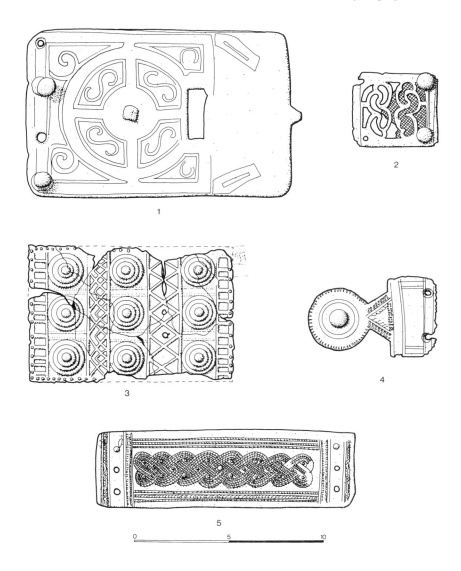

10. Decorated Republican copper-alloy fittings: 2, 4 and 5 (from Castillejo) are probably from belts; the others are from Cáceres el Viejo (1) and Renieblas camp III (3). Scale in centimetres.

Other equipment

A pickaxe (*dolabra*) was found at Numantia (figure 11, 1) and there have been numerous finds of tethering pegs (figure 11, 2), possibly used for securing animals (although it has been suggested that they may be tent pegs). Cavalry are attested by the presence of spurs as well as horses' bits.

Production

Republican soldiers were originally supposed to go on campaign with their own equipment: therefore, the different classes of legionary reflected their individual purchasing power. Polybius says the Roman soldier could buy equipment, along with food and clothing, from his *quaestor,* so we know that soldiers continued to buy their own equipment in the second century BC. There seem to have been two main ways of supplying later Republican armies: through contracts with private firms and through *officina publica* or state workshops. In 210 BC Scipio Africanus captured New Carthage, which the Carthaginians had been using as a vast arsenal. Scipio then set the craftsmen there to producing arms for him.

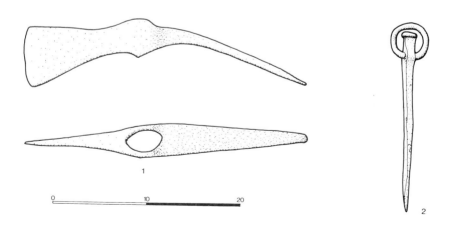

11. 1, Republican pickaxe (*dolabra*), Pena Redonda, near Numantia; 2, tethering peg with ring, Renieblas camp V. Scale in centimetres.

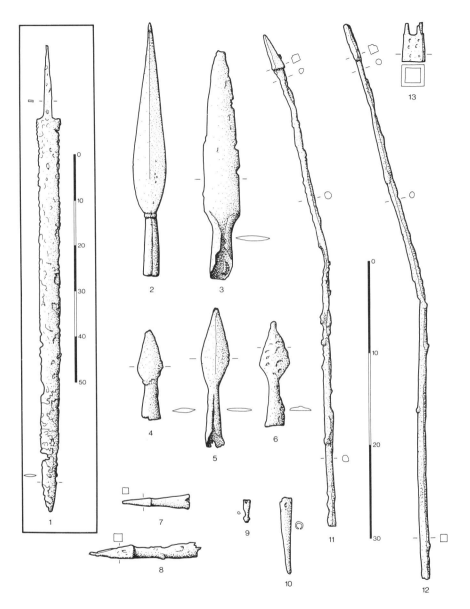

12. First-century AD weapons: 1, *spatha* (Rottweil, West Germany); 2, spearhead (Newstead, Scotland); 3-6, spearheads (Hod Hill, England); 7, catapult bolt (Hod Hill); 8, catapult bolt (Augsburg-Oberhausen, West Germany); 9, spear butt (Hod Hill); 10, spear butt (Augsburg-Oberhausen); 11, 12, *pila* (Hod Hill); 13, collet (band) from *pilum* (Dangstetten, West Germany). Scale in centimetres.

4
The first century AD

The unrest of the final century of the Republic, when soldiers' loyalty was to the warlord who paid them, meant that when Octavian (later called Augustus) gained control of the whole empire he was assured of the personal loyalty of most of the army. The army was now permanently established and increasingly began to operate in the outlying provinces of the empire for much of the time. Very soon most of the army — up to thirty legions — was stationed on the frontiers, with only a token military force, the Praetorian Guard, remaining in Rome.

The military situation was seldom static, however. Personnel, particularly centurions and equestrian and senatorial officers, were moved around and major military initiatives, such as the invasion of Britain in AD 43, necessitated the rearrangement of legions and auxiliaries over much of north-west Europe. Similar changes occurred after the civil war of AD 69, when the victorious Flavian dynasty dispersed disloyal units.

The legions were now formed of only one type of heavy infantryman but the *auxilia* contained a wide variety of specialist troops, including cavalry. Soldiers still had to purchase their own equipment. This meant that, while most of their kit may have been supplied by the army, they would be free to buy more elaborate or expensive items from private craftsmen.

Since the first century was a time of military flux in the frontier zones, many fort sites are known and a great deal of abandoned military equipment has been recovered. Much of this material is in the form of casual finds made since the end of the eighteenth century but increasingly more comes from carefully controlled archaeological excavation.

Weapons

The best preserved *pila* of any period were found in the Augustan fortress at Oberaden (West Germany). Not only the complete metal shanks and heads but also portions of the wooden shafts survived. These clearly demonstrate how the tang was riveted through a pyramidal expansion of the wooden shaft and then capped with a small iron shaft-head or collet. The iron head was usually pyramidal and both it and the shank were square in section (figure 12, 11-12). Sculptural evidence suggests that the shaft was bound below the expansion to form a handgrip. Some

13. First-century AD *gladii*: Pompeii-type blade (1) and sheath (2) (Mainz, West Germany); Mainz-type sheath (3) and blade (4), of the so-called 'Sword of Tiberius' (Mainz). Scale in centimetres.

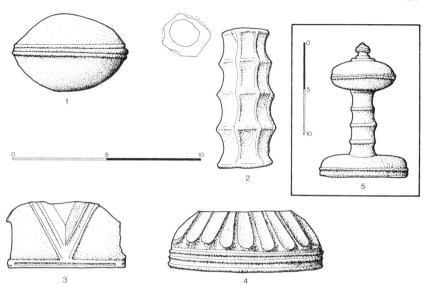

14. First-century AD sword hilts: 1, wooden pommel (Vindonissa, Windisch, Switzerland); 2, bone handgrip (Longthorpe, Cambridgeshire, England); 3, bone handguard (Rheingönheim, West Germany); 4, wooden handguard (Vindonissa); 5, complete silvered handle from Mainz-type sword (Rheingönheim). Scale in centimetres.

representations have also been thought to show the introduction of weighted *pila* in the second half of the century but no examples have yet been recovered from the archaeological record.

A similar range of spear types to that found in the Republican period is attested archaeologically (figure 12, 2-6), as well as spear butts (figure 12, 9-10). Josephus relates how each cavalryman had a spear (*lancea*) and several lighter javelins, and servants (*calones*) are shown on tombstones holding spare weapons for the rider. Auxiliary infantry are also depicted carrying two spears (*hastae*: figures 2 and 17). Analysis of the remains of wooden shafts shows that ash and hazel were commonly used.

Two types of short sword were now in use. The Mainz type, which probably closely resembled the Republican *gladius Hispaniensis*, had a tapering blade with a long point (figure 13, 4). The Pompeii type, which gradually replaced it in the second half of the first century, had a parallel-edged blade with a short point (figure 13, 1). Metallographic examination of two Pompeii-type blades has shown that they were case-hardened and did not have piled cores or employ pattern welding, as found on later swords. A variety of decorated scabbards is known for these weapons. There are three principal types of sheath for Mainz swords and two for Pompeii swords, all of which use a mixture of openwork and embossed decoration (figure 13, 2-3). Wooden, bone or ivory hilts could be used, some of these being silvered (figure 14, 5).

Auxiliary cavalry, who needed a longer reach than infantry, used a long sword, the *spatha*, derived from the Celtic long

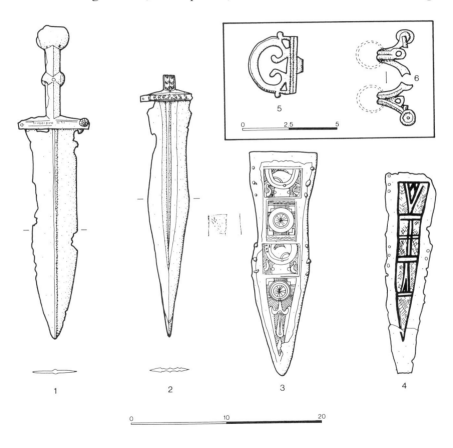

15. First-century AD daggers: 1, type A dagger (Utrecht, Netherlands); 2, type B dagger (Nijmegen, Netherlands); 3, type A sheath (Colchester, Essex, England); 4, type B sheath plate (Loughor, West Glamorgan, Wales); suspension loops from Kempten (West Germany) (5) and Dangstetten (6). Compare number 5 with buckles on figure 23, 3 and 6. Scale in centimetres.

16. First-century AD column-base from Mainz depicting two legionaries with rectangular *scuta*, a *gladius* and a *pilum*. (Landesmuseum, Mainz. Photograph: M. C. Bishop.)

sword. An example from Rottweil (West Germany) has a blade length of 860 mm (figure 12, 1).

Two main types of dagger were in use (figure 15, 1-2), the earlier again resembling its Republican predecessors in that it had a broad flat blade with a midrib and flat tang. The other form had a slim blade with a central groove and a rod tang. It has been established that some dagger blades had piled cores. Two main types of sheath were found for the *pugio*. The earlier form (type A) was made from two metal plates and lined with wood and leather, and this might be decorated on its front face with enamel or metal (gold, silver or brass) inlay (figure 15, 3). Type B sheaths (figure 15, 4) had a metal face plate but the rest was organic, so normally only the plates survive. These usually had silver-wire inlay, although there was a degree of overlap in materials and motifs between the two types of sheath. Tombstones show that both legionaries and auxiliaries wore daggers in this period and

17. First-century AD column-base from Mainz depicting an auxiliary infantryman with an oval shield and three spears. (Landesmuseum, Mainz. Photograph: M. C. Bishop.)

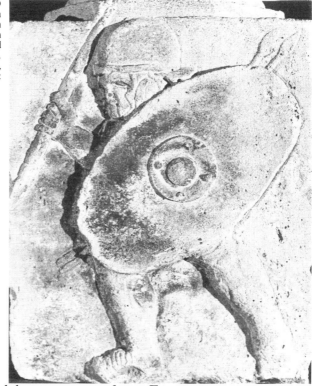

this is confirmed by a papyrus from Egypt.

Three-bladed arrowheads are known from a number of sites but the early imperial period has also produced some bone and antler ear laths from composite bows, the characteristic weapons used by archers in the Roman army. Catapult bolts are frequently found, and a hut within the hillfort at Hod Hill appears to have been used for target practice by Roman artillery. Josephus describes the effective use of stone-throwing catapults in the siege of Jerusalem.

Armour

The oval shield was changing in the late first century BC and a relief on the mausoleum of Munatius Plancus at Gaeta (Italy) shows that the curved rectangular *scutum*, so familiar from sculpture, was in use by *c.*10 BC. Auxiliary troops were equipped with flat shields, which could be oval (figure 17), hexagonal or, occasionally, rectangular. All that normally survives is fragments of the brass edge-binding (figure 18, 3), although some pieces of a shield were found under the rampart of the fort at Doncaster (South Yorkshire, England). Shield bosses were normally hemispherical (figure 18, 2). When not in use, shields were protected

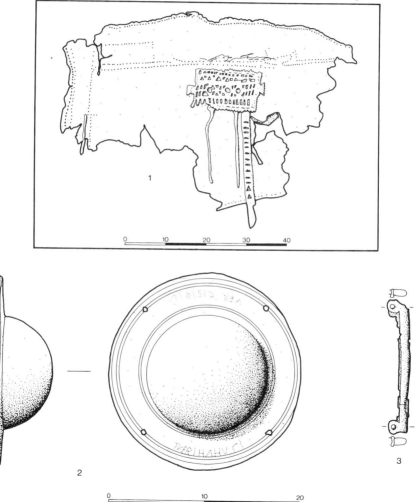

18. First-century AD shield fittings: 1, leather cover (Vindonissa); 2, copper-alloy shield boss with punched ownership inscription (Zwammerdam, Netherlands); 3, copper-alloy shield binding (Risstissen, West Germany). Scale in centimetres.

by a removable leather cover: fragments of these have been found (figure 18, 1).

Mail armour continued in use in this period and was worn by both auxiliaries and legionaries, although a more refined version — with small scales attached (and possibly called *lorica plumata*) — is sometimes recovered. Small portions of mail occur from time to time on sites, as do the fastening hooks (figure 19, 1). Scale armour is also found (figure 19, 2) but neither *hamata* nor *squamata* leave as much evidence in the archaeological record as the so-called '*lorica segmentata*' (this name was not used by the Romans but invented during the Renaissance). This was formed of bands of iron fastened together on the inside by strips of leather and fastened at the front and back with laces, buckles and straps. These fittings, which were usually made of thin brass sheet, were very fragile and often broke, which is why they are so frequently found by archaeologists (figure 20).

A number of different types of helmet were current in the first century. The Montefortino type continued from the Republican period but most helmet bowls were now spun rather than beaten. A Celtic derivative, the Coolus (or 'jockey-cap') type, was made of copper alloy. Imperial-Gallic helmets appear also to have had Celtic origins and were made from either copper alloy or iron. They are easily recognised by the stylised eyebrows on the helmet bowl and some pieces are extremely elaborately decorated with bosses. Imperial-Italic helmets were similar to their Imperial-Gallic counterparts but were generally more crudely made and lacked the eyebrows. All iron helmets had to be beaten out. Cavalry helmets (often elaborately embossed) can now be distinguished, their cheek-pieces completely covering the ears (figure 21, 5). Many of the best preserved first-century helmets

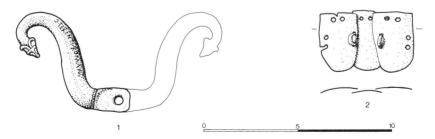

19. First-century AD armour: 1, mail fastener with punched ownership inscription (Neuss, West Germany): 2, three scales of *lorica squamata* (Moers-Asberg, West Germany). Scale in centimetres.

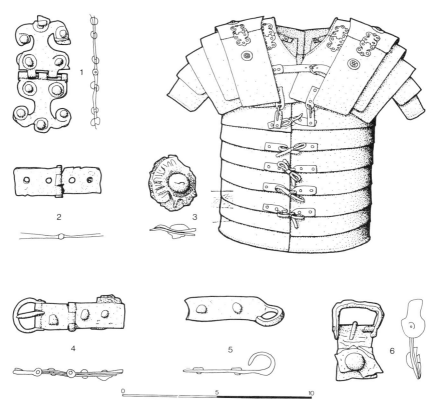

20. First-century AD *'lorica segmentata'*: reconstruction of Corbridge (Northumberland, England) type B cuirass with fittings from Risstissen. 1, Lobate hinge; 2, hinged strap fitting; 3, decorated boss and rivet; 4, hinged buckle; 5, tie-hook; 6, iron buckle from type A cuirass. Scale in centimetres.

have come from rivers, particularly the Rhine and Danube.

There is no evidence that the Romans used 'parade' armour for ceremonial occasions, although it has been suggested that some of the flimsier defences were for this purpose. 'Sports' armour (figure 22), on the other hand, was used by cavalry to protect them and their horses during the *Hippika Gymnasia*, an elaborate ritual where they practised manoeuvring and missile handling.

Ordinary soldiers did not normally wear greaves, but tombstones show the centurions did.

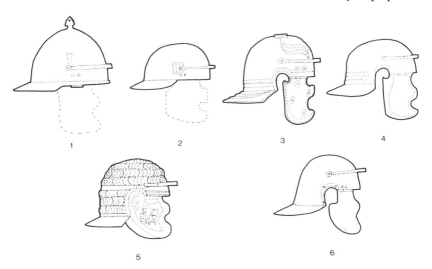

21. First-century AD helmets: 1, Montefortino type (Mainz); 2, Coolus type (London); 3, Imperial-Gallic type (Weisenau, West Germany); 4, Imperial-Italic type (Cremona, Italy); 5, cavalry helmet (Koblenz, West Germany); 6, 'auxiliary' infantry helmet (Mainz). Not to scale.

22. First-century AD type cavalry 'sports' helmet (Ribchester, Lancashire, England). (Photograph and copyright: British Museum.)

Personal equipment

Large numbers of belt-plates are known for this period, most of which were very finely decorated, with either niello inlay or embossed designs (figure 23, 1-2 and 4-5). All of them used decorative motifs derived almost entirely from classical art. These were matched by a variety of buckle types (figure 23, 3, 6 and 9). Tombstones show that belts were worn in pairs, one for the sword and one for the dagger, and these were frequently crossed 'cowboy fashion'. Later in the century it became more common to wear only one belt, and at about this time belt-plates became broader: this change may have been brought about by the introduction of *'lorica segmentata'*. The belt of this period is frequently called the *cingulum militare*, but literary and papyrological evidence suggests that it was actually known as the *balteus*, the former term referring to the belt of the later Empire.

The 'apron' that is such a prominent feature of figured tombstones seems to have developed from the free end of a belt, ornamented with studs and finished with a terminal. By the middle of the century the 'apron' had acquired as many as eight straps, each with sixteen studs. One such strap, complete with studs and terminal, was found at Mainz (West Germany; figure 23, 16). The marine found on the beach at Herculaneum was wearing a complete 'apron'. The 'apron' probably did not offer much protection to the soldier's lower abdomen, as some have suggested, but was worn rather for visual effect and the jingling noise it made.

Two types of cloak were in use by soldiers: the *sagum* and the *paenula* (figure 2). The *sagum* was draped round the shoulder and fastened with a brooch, usually on the right shoulder. The *paenula* was more like a poncho, in that it had an opening in the centre, and the soldier would put it over his head. Both types of cloak were worn by legionaries and auxiliaries. First-century military footwear consisted of the *caliga*, a hobnailed boot made from three pieces of pig leather laced up the front. Fragments are known from a number of sites but complete boots were found at Mainz (figure 24) and Valkenburg (Netherlands).

Other equipment

Cavalry equipment from this period has survived in large quantities and reconstruction work has suggested ways in which it worked. In the mid 1980s the Roman saddle was reconstructed (figure 25, 1), using the evidence of leather covers and copper-alloy horns, and this suggests that Roman cavalry, who did not

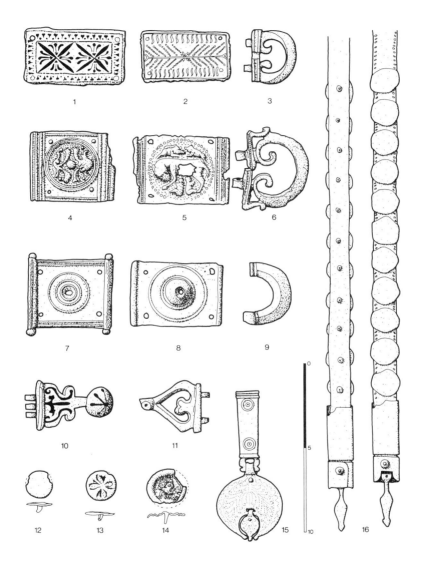

23. First-century AD belt and 'apron' fittings: belt-plates from Colchester (1), Hod Hill (2, 4, 7-8), Risstissen (5); buckles from London (3), Risstissen (6), Vindonissa (9); dagger frogs from Hod Hill (10, 11); studs from Sheepen, near Colchester (12), Colchester (13), St Albans (Hertfordshire, England) (14); 'apron' terminal from Tekija (Yugoslavia) (15); 'apron' strap from Mainz (16). Scale in centimetres.

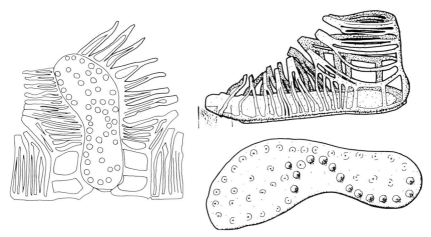

24. First-century AD boots (*caligae*), from Mainz.

have stirrups, were nevertheless securely seated. Harness straps were decorated with mounts, *phalerae* (discs) and pendants and worked in a similar way to modern riding tack. Large *phalerae* acted as junctions between the main straps (figure 26, 1 and 3). An extensive collection of copper-alloy harness fittings, decorated with silver foil and niello inlay, was dredged from the Rhine at Doorwerth.

Roman cavalry did not, apparently, use horseshoes (since they usually travelled off the road) but 'hippo sandals' (a type of

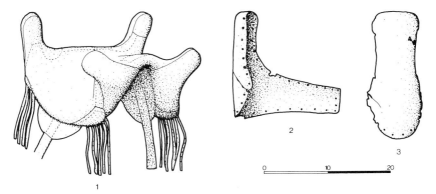

25. 1, Peter Connolly's reconstruction of the Roman saddle; copper-alloy saddle horns (Rottweil), rear (2) and front (3). Scale in centimetres.

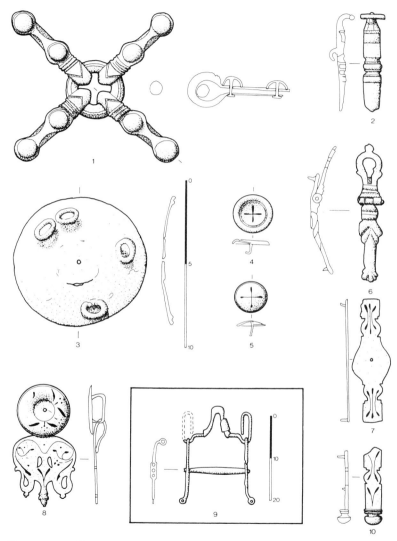

26. First-century AD cavalry harness fittings: 1, ring junction (Birten, West Germany); 2, male strap fastener (Chichester, West Sussex, England); 3, rear view of junction *phalera* (Corbridge); 4, 5, decorated studs (Fremington Hagg, North Yorkshire, England); 6, female strap fastener (Longthorpe); 7, decorative strap mount (Fremington Hagg); 8, decorative *phalera* and pendant (Fremington Hagg); 9, iron curb bit (Augsburg-Oberhausen); 10, strap terminal (Fremington Hagg). Scales in centimetres.

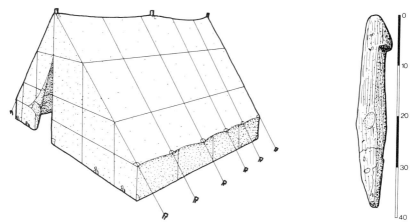

27. Reconstruction of leather tent with wooden tent peg (Velsen, Netherlands). Scale in centimetres.

temporary shoe) are occasional finds at military sites, although the precise function of these is unknown. A wide range of horse bits, including snaffle and curb types, was used on Roman horses.

Examples of the tools used by the army, such as the pickaxe *(dolabra)*, entrenching tool *(ligo)* and turf-cutter are known. Double-ended wooden stakes, sometimes mistakenly called *pila muralia*, were probably used to form *chevaux de frise* type barriers, which could be used to obstruct the entrances to camps. Several hundred such stakes were found at Oberaden. Pieces of tent panel come from a number of waterlogged sites and wooden

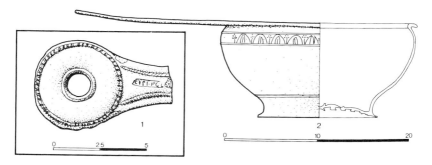

28. First-century AD *patera*: 1, stamped handle (Chester, Cheshire, England); 2, complete vessel (South Shields). Scales in centimetres.

tent pegs are occasionally found (figure 27). The soldier would use a bronze (not brass) pan or *patera* (figure 28) for cooking while on campaign and stamps on these show that they were normally manufactured in Italy and not by the army.

Production

The little evidence available for this period suggests that the army manufactured most of its required equipment itself, using the facilities available in its workshops (*fabricae*) and the manpower in the unit. Private craftsmen may have produced elaborately decorated items, such as a Mainz-type sword sheath from Vindonissa, which bears an inscription showing that it was made in Lugdunum (Lyons, France) by C. Coelius Venustus. He was clearly a Roman citizen: such private craftsmen may have been retired legionaries.

The army recycled damaged equipment as scrap, so cutting down its need for raw materials. When the army abandoned a fort site, it sometimes left scrap behind and this is probably how much of the excavated material came to be in the ground. When a soldier retired he sold his equipment back to the army and it would be reissued. This explains why some helmets bear punched inscriptions from several owners.

Much of the copper-alloy equipment used by the army of this period was made of brass (copper and zinc), known as *orichalcum* (an alloy also used by Augustus for low-denomination coinage), whereas bronze (copper and tin) seems to have been favoured before and after the first century.

5
The second century AD

Material characteristic of the latter half of the first century AD seems to have continued in use until at least the time of Hadrian. The collection of material known as the Corbridge Hoard, found in Northumberland, England, which can be dated to the beginning of the second quarter of the century, contains equipment that would not have been out of place fifty years earlier.

When the century began the Dacian Wars were still in progress and the Adamklissi monument suggests that some extraordinary measures had become necessary during this conflict: legionaries are depicted wearing greaves (something they had given up in the early Republic) and segmental armguards similar to those worn by gladiators. It has been suggested that the Dacian *falx*, a vicious scythe-like weapon, was responsible for this, as it may have been for the introduction of cross-bracing on helmet bowls.

The biographer of the emperor Hadrian relates that, as part of his general interest in the army, the emperor improved the soldiers' arms and equipment. However, it is in the Antonine period that a major change becomes apparent. In the west, at least, openwork decoration employing La Tène Celtic motifs began to appear, along with the use of enamel inlay, which replaced niello. The army was becoming sedentary and, since most of it was based in Celtic areas and was probably beginning to recruit locally, it is hardly surprising to find Celtic influence emerging. In the middle of the century the costly Marcommanic Wars of Marcus Aurelius led to fresh (and eventually influential) contacts with steppe peoples across the Danube. The century ended in the civil war that brought Septimius Severus to power.

Weapons

The *pilum* is found in second-century contexts; there are examples from a well at Bar Hill on the Antonine Wall, Scotland, probably dating to the abandonment of the fort in the 160s. A relief from the neighbouring fort at Croy Hill shows three legionaries with this weapon (figure 29, 1). Examples of *pilum* heads from Newstead (Borders) in lowland Scotland are quite long by comparison with earlier examples, up to 70 mm in length.

The infantry *gladius* was still in use in the first half of the second century, to judge from excavated scabbard fittings. The

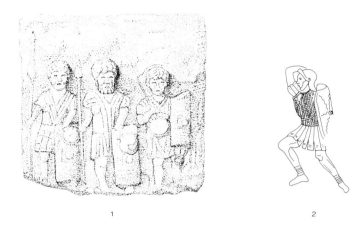

29. 1, Three legionaries on a relief from Croy Hill (Strathclyde, Scotland); 2, legionary from repoussé decoration on a helmet from Nawa (Syria).

30. Second-century swords and fittings: scabbard-slide, from Hadrian's Wall turret 50b (1); peltate chape, from Hadrian's Wall turret 35a (2); ring-pommel swords, from Denklingen, West Germany (3), unknown origin (4). Scales in centimetres.

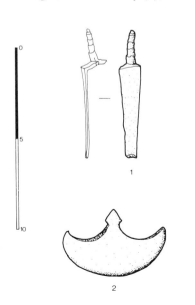

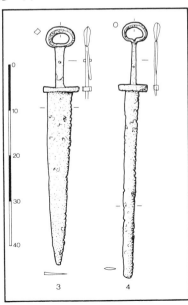

31. Copper-alloy legionary shield boss with niello inlay and punched decoration and ownership inscription (river Tyne at South Shields). Scale in centimetres.

longer *spatha*, the cavalryman's sword, continued in service. The Nawa (Syria) burial contained both a long sword of 710 mm and a shorter one of 500 mm. However, finds from Newstead and the turrets on Hadrian's Wall indicate that scabbards were beginning to change. Peltate chapes are now found, as well as scabbard-slides (figure 30, 1-2), illustrating the form of sword carriage that was to become standard in the third century (with the sword on the left, suspended from a broad decorated baldric). Ring-pommel swords were introduced in this period (figure 30, 3-4). Reliefs show soldiers wearing both the *paenula* and the ring-pommel sword (but still on the right hip at this stage).

The *pugio* continued in use into the second century, as is shown

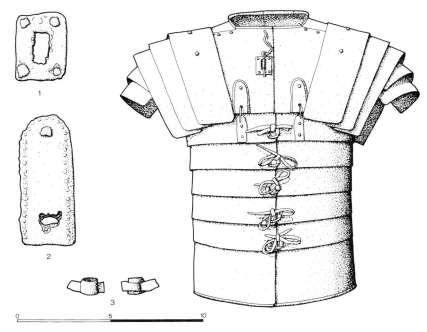

32. Later second-century *'lorica segmentata'*: reconstruction Newstead-type cuirass with fittings from Newstead; 1, breast and back-plate fastening; 2, eyelet strip from hook-and-eye fastening; 3, tie-loop. Scale in centimetres.

by the tombstone of C. Castricius Victor from Budapest. This is further supported by a dagger from Buciumi (Romania), in the new province of Dacia, and a dagger handle from Bar Hill.

Three-bladed arrowheads, as well as ear laths, were found at Bar Hill, indicating the presence of archers. In addition an open-headed fire arrow was recovered.

Armour

No shields have survived from this century but the Croy Hill relief and the figures on an embossed helmet from Nawa (figure 29) demonstrate that the curved rectangular *scutum* was still in use. This is confirmed by the decorated shield boss found in the river Tyne near South Shields fort, England (figure 31). This belonged to Junius Dubitatus of the *legio VIII Augusta*, which probably visited Britain during the reign of Hadrian.

The Adamklissi monument depicts legionaries using scale and mail, in contrast to Trajan's Column, where they are equipped with '*lorica segmentata*' (figure 1). The hoard from Corbridge shows that essentially the same form of segmental armour was being used in the first part of the second century as in the first century. However, later in the second century, when the fort at Newstead was abandoned, some pieces of '*lorica segmentata*' were thrown down the well of the headquarters building. This was a new, simplified form of the cuirass, with fewer fittings that could be damaged (figure 32). A new type of scale armour appeared during this century, on which, instead of the scale being wired only to its horizontal neighbours and then sewn to a backing, it was now wired to the one above and the one below as

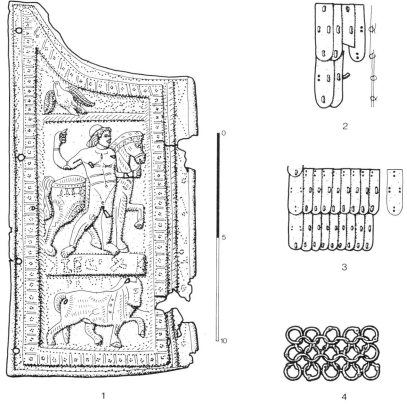

33. Second-century armour: 1, decorated breastplate from mail or scale armour, belonging to *legio X Gemina* (Muşov, Czechoslovakia); 2, 3, semi-rigid scale armour (Corbridge); 4, mail (Newstead). Scale in centimetres.

34. Second-century helmets: 1, Imperial-Gallic (Berzovia, Romania); 2, Imperial-Italic (Hebron, Israel). Not to scale.

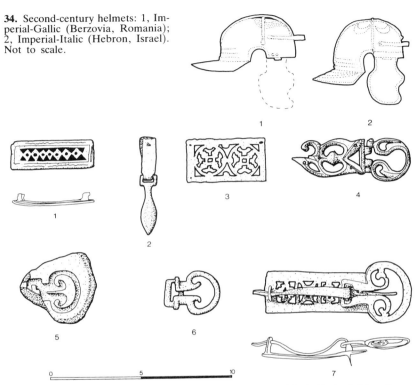

35. Second-century belt fittings: 1, enamel-inlaid belt-plate (Corbridge); 2, hinged strap terminal (Hadrian's Wall turret 50b); 3, openwork belt-plate (Hadrian's Wall turret 52a); 4, openwork belt-plate and buckle (Newstead); 5, mould for buckle (Tibiscum, Romania); 6, buckle of similar type to that produced from number 5 (South Shields); 7, rear view of openwork belt-plate and buckle (Osterburcken, West Germany). Scale in centimetres.

well. Small decorated breastplates are associated with both *lorica squamata* and *hamata* and these have frequently been identified as 'parade' or 'sports' armour but legionary examples are known from north of the Danube (figure 33, 1) in contexts relating to the Marcommanic Wars.

Examples of segmental armguards have been excavated at Carnuntum (Austria) and, possibly, at Newstead (although the latter pieces have been reconstructed as a thighguard).

An Imperial-Gallic helmet with the cross-bracing depicted on Trajan's Column (figure 1) and the Adamklissi monument has been found at Berzovia (Romania); this looks as if it may have been a field modification (figure 34, 1). Another helmet (this time an Imperial-Italic example), probably from a cave near Hebron (Israel) and possibly associated with the Bar Kochba Revolt of AD 132, also features cross-pieces. In general terms the neckguards on helmets seem to have become deeper, offering increased protection to the wearer.

Some pieces of cavalry 'sports' armour were present in the burial at Nawa, including eyeguards for a horse and two decorated helmets, one of which had its face-mask. A mid second-century helmet mask was found in a barrack block at Echzell (West Germany).

Personal equipment

As was mentioned earlier, enamel-inlaid equipment was introduced on a large scale during the second century. This was particularly evident on belt-plates (figure 35, 1). Openwork belt-plates are also found for the first time and hinged strap terminals are known from the turrets on Hadrian's Wall (figure 35, 2-4). The new kind of baldric, such a familiar feature of third-century equipment, was introduced in the second half of the century, accompanying the change from wearing the sword on the right to the left hip. A virtually complete set of belt and baldric fittings was recorded in a grave at Lyons, thought to date to the battle of Lugdunum (AD 197), when Septimius Severus came to power (figure 36).

The Croy Hill relief shows the *paenula* still in use (figure 29, 1), although it seems to be the latest provincial military representation of this garment. At some point soldiers seem to have adopted everyday civilian footwear (*calcei*) and *caligae* fell out of use.

Other equipment

The material from Bar Hill included a leather bag and various pieces of tent panels but there were also a number of tools. One of these was a hammer-head bearing a scratched inscription showing that it came from the century of Ebutius. A double-ended stake (probably part of a *chevaux de frise* barrier) from a well at Welzheim (West Germany) has been shown by dendrochronology (tree-ring dating) to have been felled in the middle of the second century.

Production

It was probably at this stage in the development of the imperial army that the production of equipment by the army itself began to spread. Auxiliary units could copy pieces of

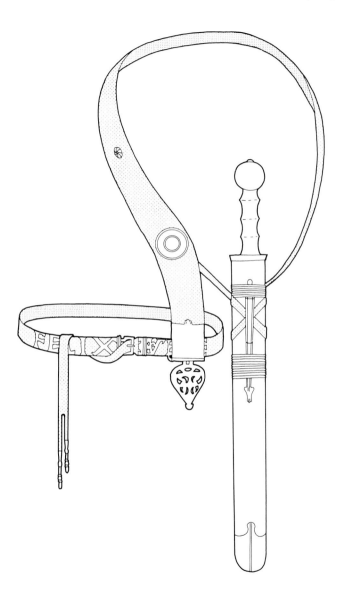

36. Reconstruction of late second-century belt and baldric using the fittings from the burial at Lyons (France). Not to scale.

equipment by taking impressions and forming moulds: designs could be spread by direct imitation. Private manufacture may also have become more common but the army was probably still responsible for the bulk of its equipment production. A papyrus of the second or third century from Egypt records the involvement of auxiliaries, legionaries and civilians in producing arms and armour in a legionary *fabrica*. Outside the fort at Tibiscum (Romania) a workshop of the second half of the second century has produced moulds for military equipment (figure 35, 5), although these were simple pieces, easy to copy.

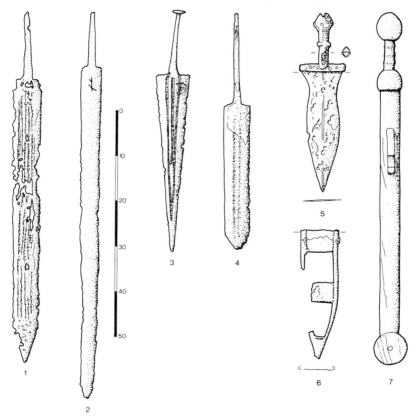

37. Third-century swords and daggers: 1, inlaid long sword (Lorch/Enns, Austria); 2, long sword (Straubing, West Germany); 3, 4, short swords (Künzing, West Germany); 5, dagger, and 6, sheath (Künzing); 7, long sword and ivory sheath (Khisfine, Syria). Scale in centimetres.

6
The third century AD

This period was marked by serious upheavals and defeats for an empire which almost did not survive. Major disasters in the east meant that many units simply ceased to exist. The abandonment of forts in Dacia (approximately modern Romania) and parts of Germany in the third quarter of the century provides cut-off dates for equipment found in these areas.

While there was little basic organisational change, new enemies and new strategic problems led to an increased need for the static frontier units to send off detachments and, especially under Gallienus (AD 253-68), new types of units, notably light cavalry, provided some mobile reserve. The extension of citizenship to all free inhabitants of the empire reduced legionary status to the same level as that of auxiliaries, while frontier policing functions rendered the equipment of both troop types virtually indistinguishable.

The frontiers were not impervious barriers to equipment or influences moving inwards or outwards. Interaction with steppe peoples across the Danube and the politico-military importance of the Illyrians (from an area in modern Yugoslavia and Hungary) led to the spread of particular equipment types and funerary practices from the Danube region. The existence of the Roman empire profoundly affected neighbouring peoples. Along the Rhine and Danube supra-tribal blocks formed, better equipped than hitherto with Roman or Roman-influenced arms and armour. In the east, Sassanid Persians continued traditional Mesopotamian armoured horse-archer warfare but adopted Roman siege technology, especially artillery.

Weapons

Cavalry and infantry swords were now always worn on the soldier's left hip, suspended from a wide baldric. *Spatha* finds (figure 37, 1-2) fall into a proportionally long, narrow Straubing-Nydam blade type (about 66-79 cm long, 4-4.6 cm wide) and a broader Lauriacum type (about 65.5 cm long, 6.5 cm wide). A number of blades bore inlaid figural decoration (figure 37, 1-2) and bone or ivory grip assemblies were sometimes employed. Short swords were still in use, judging from weapons found at Künzing (West Germany; figure 37, 3-4) and tombstone representations, but *spathae* largely replaced *gladii* in infantry use over

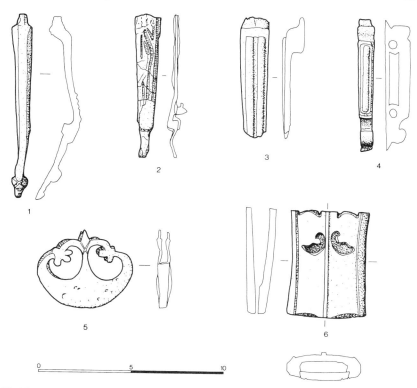

38. Third-century scabbard-slides and chapes: 1, scabbard-slide of copper alloy (Colchester); 2, iron scabbard-slide (Vindolanda, Northumberland, England); 3, bone scabbard-slide (South Shields); 4, ivory scabbard-slide (South Shields); 5, peltate chape (Richborough, Kent, England); 6, bone 'box chape' (Colchester). Scale in centimetres.

the century. Ring-pommel swords continued in use. Bone and copper-alloy model swords depict round chapes, ring pommels and slides.

Scabbard fittings included flat circular chapes of copper alloy or iron, some richly inlaid with metal or niello. Peltate bronze chapes continued through from the second century (figure 38, 5). Trapezoidal bone 'box chapes' are commonly found in Britain and Germany (figure 38, 6). A fine leather baldric from Vimose (Denmark), 8 cm wide and 118.5 cm long (figure 39, 7), together with tombstone representations (figure 40, 2), explains a common method of sword suspension. The narrower end of the baldric was attached to the outer face of the scabbard using an iron, copper-alloy, ivory or bone scabbard-slide (figure 38, 1-4). A plain or openwork copper-alloy *phalera* near the other end of the baldric was fastened to the scabbard by an eye and tie, so that the

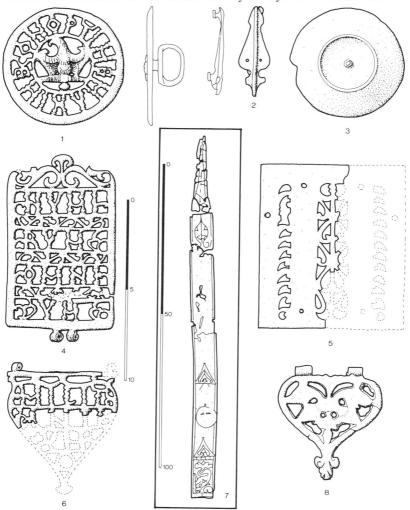

39. Third-century baldric fittings and strap mount: 1, *phalera* (Carlisle, Cumbria, England); 2, *beneficiarius* lance strap mount (South Shields); 3, *phalera* (the Saalburg, West Germany); 4, hinged terminal plate, 5, strap mount, and 6, hinged pendant (Zugmantel, West Germany); 7, leather baldric (Vimose, Denmark); 8, hinged pendant (Vindolanda). Scale in centimetres.

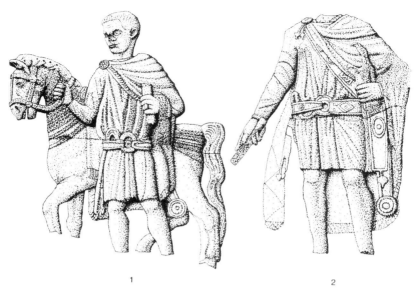

40. Third-century figured tombstones, from Rome, of unknown soldiers with ring-buckles.

broader belt end could hang down alongside the sword. A copper-alloy plate with a hinged terminal was often attached to this end (figure 39, 4, 6 and 8). Openwork *phalerae* and terminal plates sometimes carry the motto OPTIME MAXIME CON(SERVA) NUMERVM OMNIVM MILITANTIVM ('Jupiter, Best and Greatest, protect the company of all serving soldiers').

Daggers from Künzing, London and elsewhere demonstrate continuity in use (figure 37, 5-6) but third-century blades were much larger than those of earlier periods (about 280 cm long and 92 cm wide). The Künzing and London sheaths were bound with copper-alloy guttering.

Pilum heads from the Caerleon (Gwent, Wales) rampart-back store suggest continual use of this weapon by some legionary troops (figure 41, 1-2). Tombstone depictions attest employment of heavily weighted *pila* by praetorians (soldiers belonging to the imperial bodyguard). However, legionary *stelae* show one or two spears or javelins being carried, some with barbed heads, reflecting the range of shafted weapons in use by the legions. In general, third-century spearheads differ little from those of earlier periods (figure 41, 3-4 and 7-8), although examples from

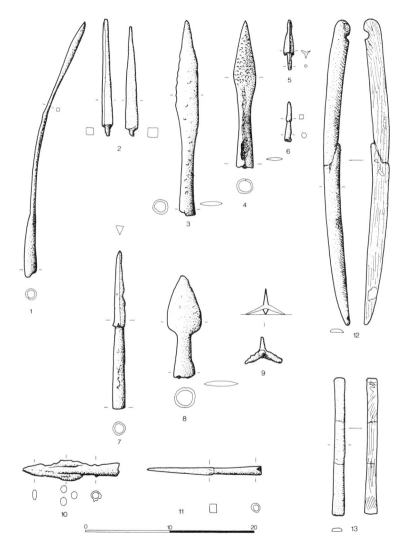

41. Third-century weapons: 1, *pilum*, 2, *pilum* heads, and 3, spearhead (Caerleon, Gwent, Wales); 4, spearhead (Künzing); 5, three-bladed, and 6, square-sectioned arrowheads (the Saalburg); 7, triangular-sectioned spearhead (Künzing); 8, spearhead, and 9, caltrop (Caerleon); 10, fire-bolt head (Dura-Europos, Syria); 11, catapult bolt-head (Künzing); 12, antler ear lath, and 13, grip lath from composite bow (Caerleon). Scale in centimetres.

Caerleon are quite narrow. A new form, consisting of a wickedly barbed head and a long shank (figure 52, 8), may have come into use now or later and represents either a *pilum* derivative or the influence of Germanic weapons like those from Danish bog deposits. Copper-alloy appliqués also occur in the form of miniature *beneficiarius* lance heads (figure 39, 2).

The Caerleon assemblage contains socketed three- or four-bladed arrowheads, derived from earlier tanged types, and a large collection of bone and antler composite bow ear and grip laths, many still unfinished (figure 41, 12-13). Socketed arrowheads, possibly of late third-century date, also occur at Corbridge. Artillery of this period is represented by a catapult, with torsion frame and washer fittings, found at Hatra (Iraq) and associated with the city's fall to the Sassanids in the mid century. Well preserved wooden catapult bolts with wooden vanes (or flights) were found at Dura. In addition to the normal form of iron bolt-heads, an open fire-bolt head also survived (figure 41, 10).

Caltrops from Caerleon represent a common anti-personnel device used across the front of an army in battle and around fort defences to disrupt besieging assaults (figure 41, 9). Four iron spikes joined at the base project at angles which ensure that one point is always vertical.

Armour

The *'lorica segmentata'* probably did not survive the second century. *Loricae hamatae* were worn by Roman soldiers in the Dura siege mine and mail occurs in the late third-century Caerleon equipment store. A well preserved portion of a *lorica squamata* was found in the Severan legionary base at Carpow (Tayside, Scotland), probably in association with the abandonment of the site. It has copper-alloy scales attached to each other by wire and to a surviving linen textile backing by linen cord. Large numbers of copper-alloy scales were found throughout Dura. Tombstones habitually depicted the deceased unarmoured (figure 40) but there is no evidence to suggest that infantry were less heavily armoured than in earlier periods.

In Tower 19 at Dura two iron and copper-alloy scale horse trappers were found with surviving fabric backings (figure 42). These unique finds represent the heavy armour commonly employed by cavalry on the eastern frontier as protection against arrows (figure 43).

A third-century cavalry helmet from Heddernheim (West

42. One of the Dura scale trappers soon after its discovery. From Rostovtzeff *et al*, 1936.

Germany) has a low-backed iron bowl, wide and steeply angled neckguard and ear-covering flanged cheek-pieces (figure 44, 1). Cavalry 'sports' helmets are also well represented by another Heddernheim helmet, this one tinned, with a metal eagle-headed crest, a narrow neck flange and a one-piece face-mask which covers the front and sides of the head, leaving a T-shaped opening for eyes, nose and mouth (figure 45). A sports mask of a different type, with a high comb of hair, was found in a site abandonment hoard from Straubing (West Germany), together with greaves and hinged copper-alloy embossed horse chamfrons.

Very few surviving third-century helmets continue the earlier infantry developments. A fine copper-alloy example from Niedermörmter (West Germany) may be Severan and has a very low and wide neckguard (figure 44, 2). An iron helmet with bowl cross-pieces comes from Theilenhofen (West Germany; figure 44, 3). Infantry tombstones depict helmets with low-backed bowls and pointed peaks, reminiscent of cavalry helmets, and it may be that these forms were adopted by infantry. Thus helmet fragments from Dura and a copper-alloy helmet from Buch (West Germany; figure 44, 4), with steeply angled neckguard and enclosing cheek-pieces, may be attributable to infantry.

Both domed circular shield bosses and domed *umbones* with rectangular plates in iron and copper alloy were found at Dura. One complete curved rectangular shield, 108 cm high and 83 cm wide, and other fragmentary examples provide evidence for the continuity of this form (figure 46). Construction consisted of three layers of glued strips of plane wood, the inner and outer layers laid horizontally, the middle layer vertically. The back was braced by wooden strips and the whole shield was covered with parchment. It was then painted and a layer of parchment was glued to the front. The edges were bound with leather and decorative motifs and figures were painted on the face. Five almost complete dished oval shields were also found at Dura,

43. Graffito of armoured cavalryman from Dura-Europos.

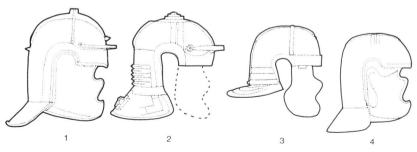

44. Third-century helmets: 1, Heddernheim (West Germany); 2, Niedermörmter (West Germany); 3, Theilenhofen (West Germany); 4, Buch (West Germany). Not to scale.

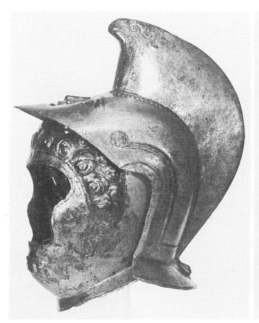

45. (Above left) Third-century cavalry 'sports' helmet (Heddernheim). (Photograph and copyright: Museum für Vor- und Frühgeschichte, Frankfurt am Main.)

46. (Above right) Reconstructed legionary *scutum* (Dura-Europos). The lion may be a legionary emblem. (From Rostovtzeff *et al*, 1936.)

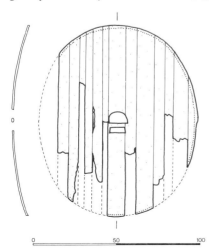

47. Oval shield V (Dura-Europos). Scale in centimetres.

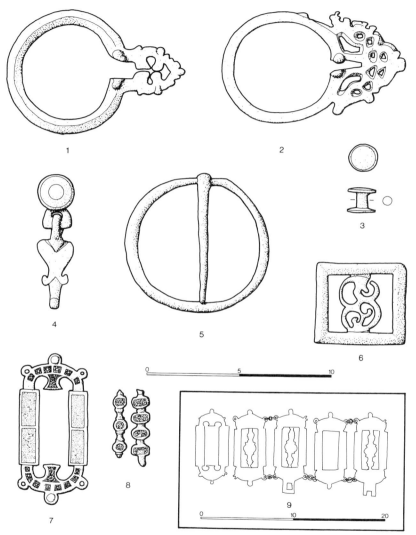

48. Third-century belt fittings: 1, 2, decorated copper-alloy ring-buckles (Intercisa, Hungary); 3, stud, and 4, strap terminal (South Shields); 5, plain iron ring-buckle (Gheyta, Egypt); 6, rectangular buckle (Pfünz, West Germany); 7, enamelled belt-plate (Dorchester, Dorset, England); 8, central bars from enamelled belt-plates (Caerleon); 9, enamelled belt-plates showing orientation (South Shields). Scale in centimetres.

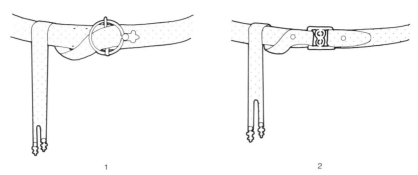

49. Reconstructions of third-century belts: 1, ring-buckle with tongue; 2, rectangular buckle. Not to scale.

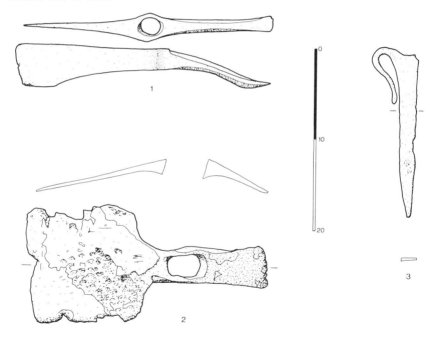

50. Third-century equipment: 1, pickaxe (*dolabra*); 2, entrenching tool (*ligo*); 3, tethering or tent peg (all from Künzing). Scale in centimetres.

107-18 cm high and 92-7 cm wide (figure 47). They were constructed of twelve to fifteen poplar-wood planks glued edgewise and running longitudinally. The edges were bound with stitched leather strips: it appears that shields were no longer edged with bronze guttering. They were richly painted with figural decoration. All the oval and rectangular shields had a horizontal central handgrip and perhaps belonged to infantry troops. Oval shields were commonly depicted on tombstones, as were a few rectangular boards. Very large round shields are sometimes seen carried by cavalrymen.

Personal equipment

Plain iron or copper-alloy rings, or adjustable decorated copper-alloy examples, with or without a tongue, have been found in positions in inhumations which suggested waist-belt fastening (figure 48, 1-2 and 5). Tombstones commonly depict ring-buckles worn by both infantry and cavalry (figure 40) and demonstrate the use of studs to hold belt ends passed through the ring (figure 49, 2). One end of the belt often hangs down from the wearer's right hip and numerous hinged copper-alloy terminals (figure 48, 4), for example a pair in a burial at Lyons, were attached to the split ends (figure 36). Alternative forms of rectangular buckle were used with this pass-through method (figure 48, 6). Tombstones also suggest the application of purely decorative copper-alloy plates to the belt. Bronze letters spelling VTERE FELIX ('Use with good luck') were applied to belts from the end of the second century onwards.

Soldiers appear on tombstones in long-sleeved tunics, *sagum*-type cloaks fastened by disc-brooches, with either bare legs or tight-fitting trousers. Paintings from Dura and Egypt suggest that tunics were commonly white with decorative purple embroidery and that cloaks were worn. Clothing may have changed little in cut and decoration into the fifth century.

Other equipment

A number of *dolabrae*, entrenching tools and tethering or tent pegs were found in the ironwork hoard from Künzing (figure 50, 1-3), demonstrating that auxiliaries were now fully involved in engineering tasks.

Cavalry equipment of the third century had changed considerably from that of the early empire. In general it was far simpler, using *phalera* junctions through which the leather harness was looped, thus avoiding the need for fragile fittings joining the strap to the junction. *Phalerae* could have external loops for straps (figure 51, 1) or, since now they were mainly openwork designs, strapping could be folded over the inner rim of a piece. Various strap mounts were used to decorate harness (figure 51, 2) and

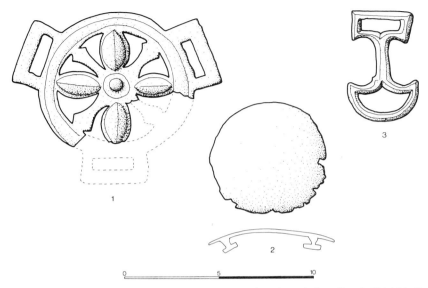

51. Third-century fittings from cavalry harness: 1, junction *phalera* (South Shields); 2, strap mount (Niederbieber, West Germany); 3, suspension loop for pendant streamer (South Shields). Scale in centimetres.

pendant streamers hung from loops suspended from the harness (figure 51, 3).

Production

Legionary *fabricae* continued in production, as the Caerleon laths suggest. At Corbridge the third-century legionary garrison was manufacturing or repairing *pila*, spearheads and arrows (although they were probably not responsible for supplying the whole of Hadrian's Wall, as was once suggested). There is also widespread evidence for the manufacture of copper-alloy items, in the form of unfinished pieces and moulds, some of it in settlements around forts in Germany, Pannonia (in modern Hungary and Yugoslavia) and Dacia.

7
The fourth and fifth centuries AD

The army that emerged from the third-century crises, reorganised and remodelled by Tetrarchic and Constantinian emperors, was very different from the forces of the principate. Old units and titles continued but unit sizes and internal organisation are now obscure and armament can often only be guessed at from the *Notitia Dignitatum*. Army expansion and new mobile field forces posed fresh problems of equipment and supply.

This transformation is reflected by radical changes and breaks in the continuity of military equipment development and by the circumstances of small-find survival, which increasingly involves inhumations and final site abandonment. Attributing change to 'barbarisation' of the army and attempting to isolate 'Germanic' elements of equipment design tend both to underestimate the long-term cultural influence of Rome on her neighbours and to ignore the fact that, in all periods, Roman military equipment was a fusion of many non-Roman traditions.

Weapons

Long swords continued in use, some with circular chapes and scabbard-slides, as the early fifth-century diptych depicting the general Stilicho and a 72 cm long *spatha* with chape from Cologne (West Germany) demonstrates (figure 52, 1). Waist-belt suspension is not often depicted in the reliable fourth-century representations of soldiers. Vegetius mentions the *semispatha*, suggesting that some form of short sword continued to be used.

Vegetius also discusses several missile weapons: the *verutum* (called *vericulum* in the past), which had a 12.5 cm long head and a 60.5 cm long shaft; the *spiculum* (called *pilum*), with a 23 cm long head and a 167.5 cm long shaft; and the *plumbata*. These last have been identified with barbed, lead-weighted heads (figure 52, 4) found, for example, at Wroxeter (Shropshire, England) and Lorch (Austria). Reconstructions of these have been made and performance experiments carried out. Spearheads from a fourth-century context at Catterick (North Yorkshire, England) are not markedly different in shape or range of types from earlier forms (figure 52, 2-3 and 5-7).

Support troops used bows, slings and staff-slings (*fustibali*). Vegetius refers to *arcuballistae*, which may have been the crossbows seen as hunting weapons on third-century Gallic

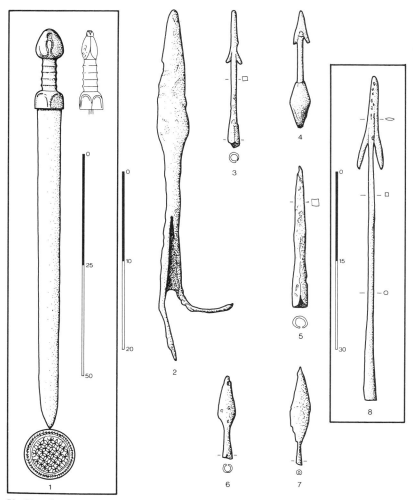

52. Fourth-century weapons: 1, *spatha* and circular chape (Cologne, West Germany); 2, 3, 5-7, spearheads (Catterick, North Yorkshire, England); 4, *plumbata* (Wroxeter, Shropshire, England); 8, barbed spearhead (Carvoran, Northumberland, England). Scales in centimetres.

reliefs. *Manuballistae* may have been used by mobile units of *ballistarii*. Small late fourth-century iron torsion frames from Gornea and Orsova (Romania) may represent such hand-held one-man *ballistae*. While heavier artillery pieces of earlier periods continued in use, a late development was the *onager*, mentioned

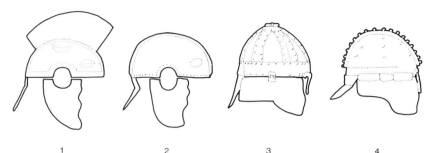

1   2   3   4

53. Fourth-century helmets: 1, 2, infantry helmets (Intercisa); 3, cavalry helmet (Deir el-Medina, Egypt); 4, cavalry helmet (Berkasovo, Yugoslavia). Not to scale.

by Ammianus and Vegetius, which used an upright throwing-arm.

Armour

The expansion of the Tetrarchic army may have caused problems in body-armour provision. However, there is good evidence that at least some infantry units were no less heavily armoured than in earlier periods. Archaising influences in contemporary art obscure this question by depicting soldiers in Hellenistic muscled cuirasses. Some forms of light cavalry were unarmoured to meet their tactical role. *Notitia* unit titles and Ammianus indicate an increased use of heavily armoured cavalry (*cataphracti* and *clibanarii*) on the Mesopotamian model.

1   2

54. 1, Representation of a fourth-century infantryman on a tombstone from Aquileia (Italy) dating to AD 352. 2, Relief from Gamzigrad (Yugoslavia) showing a fourth-century infantryman and mounted figure.

55. Fourth-century cavalry helmet (Deurne, Netherlands). (Photograph and copyright: Rijksmuseum van Oudheden, Leiden.)

Some time in the period AD 270-300 there was a complete break in helmet development and a new form of head protection is represented by two types of late third-century and fourth-century helmets. The infantry type had a bowl made up of two iron halves joined together by a strip ridge and provided with a neckguard and cheek-pieces attached to the leather or fabric lining and not hinged to the bowl (figure 53, 1-2). Some had crests of hair or of solid iron and silver foil decoration. They date to the fourth century AD and include fifteen to twenty examples from Intercisa (Hungary). A sculptural representation from Aquileia (Italy) is dated to AD 352 (figure 54, 1).

The cavalry type has an iron bowl of four to six pieces: a ridge, noseguard, neckguard and very wide cheek-pieces, which are attached to the bowl by rivets or hinges (figure 53, 3-4). Many were covered with gilded silver, which survives after the iron parts have disintegrated. Some are encrusted with glass gems and have embossed designs. Punched inscriptions give information about owners and manufacturers. This type of helmet developed under the influence of steppe forms, encountered along the Danube, and of Mesopotamian forms, represented by the Sassanid helmet in the Dura siege mine. Examples from Deurne (Netherlands; figure 55) and Berkasovo (Yugoslavia) are Constantinian, while one from a Hunnic context at Concesti (Romania) dates to the fifth century. They are represented on a Tetrarchic relief from Gamzigrad (Yugoslavia; figure 54, 2) and on the Arch of Galerius at Salonica (Greece).

All these 'ridge' helmets were technically very simple to manufacture and assemble. Their adoption was closely linked with the centralisation of armour production.

Large oval and round shields with a central boss are depicted in

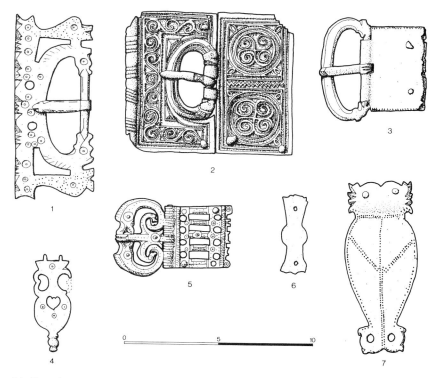

56. Fourth-century belt fittings: 1, buckle (Catterick); 2, 'chip-carved' buckle-plate (Kent); 3, buckle and plate (Winchester, Hampshire, England); 4, 'amphora-shaped' strap terminal (Richborough); 5, buckle and plate (Colchester); 6, propeller-shaped belt mount (Vindolanda); 7, strap terminal (Winchester). Scale in centimetres.

various artistic media and, with the exception of rectangular *scuta*, there was little change from third-century forms. The style of shield blazons in the *Notitia* is corroborated by sculptural and metalwork representations, although doubt has been cast on the accuracy of the former.

Personal equipment

Ring-buckles do not seem to have survived into the Tetrarchic period but wide waist-belts continued in use. Copper-alloy belt fittings are common in fourth-century to fifth-century funerary contexts and they consist of rectangular or propeller-shaped belt-stiffeners, decorative appliqué belt-plates, belt end plates, buckle plates and strap ends (figure 56). Fittings have ring-and-dot or 'chip-carved' decoration and some buckles have dolphin or horse-head details (figure 56, 1 and 5).

The broad belt was a direct development from third-century practice and decorative motifs are Roman not Germanic. A controversy surrounds the identification of wearers because of the Germanic adoption of both belt form and decoration. Finds from non-military sites, such as British villas, might suggest the use of belts as badges of militarised government office. Civil servants were technically *milites* and wore uniform. Supposed Germanic styles have been taken to indicate the presence of barbarian military settlers. However, the belts probably belonged mainly to late Roman soldiers. The three groups are not exclusive. Dating for the introduction of these belts is primarily provided by Tetrarchic tombstones and propeller-type stiffeners depicted on the Arch of Constantine (Rome; AD 315). Coins found with fittings in graves also help date these types in the fourth century.

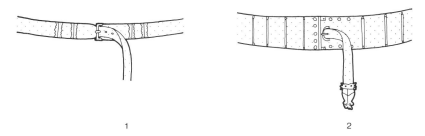

1   2

57. Reconstruction fourth-century belts: 1, Maryport (Cumbria, England) fittings; 2, Winchester material. Not to scale.

Crossbow brooches developed for *sagum* fastening. Furry flat-topped round hats were worn by soldiers of all ranks from the emperor downwards (figure 54, 2), particularly in the Tetrarchic period. Itemisation of a senior officer's clothing and equipment in the *Augustan History* (*Claudius* XIV, 5) may best suit the fourth century: two red military tunics, two cloaks, two gilded silver brooches, one gold brooch, one gilded silver belt (*balteus*), one ring with gemstones, one armlet, one torque, one gilded helmet, two gold-inlaid shields, one *lorica* (cuirass), two spears (*lanceas Herculianas*), two javelins (*aclides*), two sickles, two scythes for hay, one white part-silk tunic with Moorish purple ornament, two white undergarments, one pair of leggings (?), one *toga*, one tunic with broad stripe (?).

Production

Some fort *fabricae* continued to operate during the fourth century. A cache of eight hundred improvised tanged flat arrowheads in the *principia* (headquarters) at the fort of Housesteads (Northumberland, England), dating to the abandonment of the site, were probably produced locally. The last phase of the legionary fortress at Novae (Bulgaria) saw copper-alloy scrap collection in the *principia* and extensive bone and antler working took place within the fort at Intercisa. However, an organised imperial *fabrica* system was set up under Diocletian by *c.* AD 300. Centres for shield and armour production serving the northern and eastern frontier zones were evenly distributed, as recorded in the *Notitia* in a modified form. Heavy-armour *fabricae* corresponded with a concentration of Mesopotamian-style armoured cavalry units in the east. Artillery and archery equipment producers were located only in the west. Presumably eastern frontier cities provided their own artillery defences, while traditions of archery using composite bows were foreign to the west. Elements of the *fabrica* system survived the barbarian invasions through the fifth century, particularly in Italy and the east.

8
Glossary

Aclis: javelin.

Arcuballista: (may have been) a crossbow.

Auxiliary: soldier usually recruited from the provincial population; auxiliary units were complementary and used in a supporting role to the legions.

Baldric: belt to support a sword, worn over one shoulder.

Ballista: torsion-powered artillery piece.

Bar Kochba Revolt: Jewish rebellion in the reign of Hadrian.

Beneficiarius: soldier detached from his unit on special duties.

Beneficiarius **lance:** symbol of the status of this soldier.

Caltrop: four iron spikes joined in such a way that one always points upwards.

Case-hardened: surface of a blade made harder than its core.

Cataphractus: heavily armoured cavalryman.

Chamfron: protection or armour for the head of a horse.

Chape: scabbard fitting which houses and protects the point of the sword.

Chevaux de frise **barrier:** free-standing row of double-ended spikes, each set at 90 degrees to its neighbour.

Clibanarius: heavily armoured cavalryman.

Dacian Wars: Trajan's two campaigns north of the Danube in Dacia (approximately modern Romania).

Dioscurus: one of two mythical twins who reputedly helped Rome during a fifth-century BC battle.

Ear lath: splints glued in pairs to both ends of a composite bow to act as levers.

Eques: cavalryman.

Fabrica: workshop.

Falx: scythe-like weapon used by Dacians.

Free Germany: area outside the Roman empire, inhabited by German tribes.

Fustibalus: staff-sling.

Gladius: sword.

Hasta: infantry thrusting spear.

Hastatus: type of Republican legionary, armed with a spear.

Hoplite: heavily armed foot-soldier of ancient Greece.

Lancea: spear.

Latin Wars: struggle for control of the Latin League (an association of the people of the Italian region known as

Latium), won by Rome in 338 BC.

Legion: unit of about five thousand Roman citizen troops.

Legionaries: citizen troops, from the late Republic onwards exclusively heavy infantry.

Lorica hamata: mail armour, made from interlinking rings of iron or, occasionally, copper alloy.

Lorica plumata: (may have been) mail armour with small scales.

'Lorica segmentata': armour made from strips of iron, held together by internal strips of leather.

Lorica squamata: scale cuirass.

Manuballista: (may have been) a missile-throwing device.

Marcommanic Wars: fought in the Antonine period against tribes of German and Sarmatian origin.

Miles: soldier.

Officina publica: state workshop.

Onager: missile-throwing device using upright throwing-arm.

Pattern welding: process by which a blade is built up from several interwoven bars.

Pectorale: Republican breastplate.

Peltate: shaped like the Greek *pelta*, a crescent-shaped shield.

Piled core: with the core of a blade built up and the edges welded to it.

Pilum: heavy javelin, the metal shank of which bent upon impact.

Plumbata: barbed, lead-weighted missile head.

Praetorian: infantry soldier belonging to the imperial bodyguard.

Princeps: type of Republican legionary, armed with a *pilum*.

Pugio: dagger, worn as a side arm by soldiers.

Punic Wars: series of three wars fought against Carthage.

Quaestor: quartermaster in a Republican legion.

Scutum: shield.

Spatha: long sword of Celtic origin. In the first century AD it was normally used only by cavalry.

Spiculum: shafted missile weapon.

Spina: rib or spine on face of shield.

Spinning: process whereby a hemispherical object is made by pressing a sheet of metal down on to a rotating former.

Tang: part of a weapon passing through the handle.

Torsion frame: framework on a piece of artillery holding the hair or sinew springs that powered the firing arms.

Triarius: type of Republican legionary, armed with a *pilum*.

Umbo: shield boss.

Veles: type of Republican legionary, lightly armed.

Verutum: shafted missile weapon.

9
Museums

United Kingdom

British Museum, Great Russell Street, London WC1B 3DG. Telephone: 01-636 1555.

Corbridge Roman Site Museum, Corbridge, Northumberland NE45 5NT. Telephone: 043471 3168.

Grosvenor Museum, 27 Grosvenor Street, Chester, Cheshire CH1 2DD. Telephone: 0244 21616 or 313858.

Museum of Antiquities of the University and the Society of Antiquaries of Newcastle upon Tyne, The University, Newcastle upon Tyne NE1 7RU. Telephone: 091 2226000 extension 6844 or 6849.

Museum of London, London Wall, London EC2Y 5HN. Telephone: 01-600 3699.

National Museum of Wales, Cathays Park, Cardiff CF1 3NP. Telephone: 0222 397951.

Roman Legionary Museum, High Street, Caerleon, Gwent NP6 1AE. Telephone: 0633 423134.

Royal Museum of Scotland, Queen Street, Edinburgh EH2 1JD. Telephone: 031-225 7534.

France

Musée des Antiquités Nationales, Château de Saint-Germain, 78103 Saint-Germain-en-Laye, Yvelines.

Netherlands

Rijksmuseum van Oudheden, Rapenburg 28, 2311 EW Leiden.

Switzerland

Vindonissa Museum, Museumstrasse 1, 5200 Brugg, Aragau.

West Germany

Gäuboden und Straubing Museum, Fraunhoferstrasse 9, 8440 Straubing.

Landesmuseum Mainz, Grosse Bleiche 49-51, 6500 Mainz.

Limesmuseum, St Johanastrasse 5, 7080 Aalen.

Rheinisches Landesmuseum, Colmanstrasse 14-16, 5300 Bonn.

Römisch-Germanisches Zentralmuseum, Kurfürstliches Schloss, Ernst Ludwig Platz 2, 6500 Mainz.

Württembergisches Landesmuseum Stuttgart, Altes Schloss, 7000 Stuttgart.

10
Further reading

The published proceedings of the Roman Military Equipment Conferences contain much material that has been used in this volume.

Bishop, M. C. (editor). *The Production and Distribution of Roman Military Equipment*. BAR International Series 275, British Archaeological Reports, 1985.

Dawson, M. (editor). *Roman Military Equipment: the Accoutrements of War*. BAR International Series 336, British Archaeological Reports, 1987.

Coulston, J. C. (editor). *Military Equipment and the Identity of Roman Soldiers*. BAR International Series 394, British Archaeological Reports, 1988.

Ancient works

Josephus. *The Jewish War*. Penguin Classics, 1970. Descriptions of military equipment.

Polybius. *The Rise of the Roman Empire*. Penguin Classics, 1979. Descriptions of military equipment.

Other works

Allason-Jones, L., and Bishop, M. C. *Excavations at Roman Corbridge: the Hoard*. HBMCE Archaeological Report 7, English Heritage, 1988.

Baatz, D. 'Recent Finds of Ancient Artillery', *Britannia*, 9 (1978), 1-17.

Bishop, M. C. 'The Distribution of Military Equipment within Roman Forts of the First Century AD', *Studien zu den Militärgrenzen Roms III*, Theiss, 1986, 717-23.

Bullinger, H. *Spätantike Gürtelbeschläge*. De Tempel, 1969.

Connolly, P. *Greece and Rome at War*. Macdonald, 1981.

Coulston, J. C. 'Roman, Parthian and Sassanid Tactical Developments' in P. Freeman and D. Kennedy (editors), *The Defence of the Roman and Byzantine East*. BAR International Series 297, British Archaeological Reports, 1986, 59-75.

Curle, J. *A Roman Frontier Post and Its People*. Maclehose, 1911.

Garbsch, J. *Römische Paraderüstungen*. Beck, 1978.

von Groller, M. 'Römische Waffen', in *Römische Limes in Österreich*, volume 2. Hölder, 1911.

Hermann, F. R. 'Der Eisenhortfund aus dem Kastell Künzing', *Saalburg-Jahrbuch*, 26 (1969), 129-41.

James, S. 'Evidence from Dura-Europos for the Origins of Late Roman Helmets', *Syria*, 63 (1986), 107-34.

Junkelmann, M. *Die Legionen des Augustus*. Von Zabern, 1986.

Klumbach, H. *Römische Helme aus Niedergermanien*. Rheinland, 1974.

Klumbach, H. *Spätrömische Gardehelme*. Beck, 1973.

Marsden, E. W. *Greek and Roman Artillery. Historical Development*. Oxford, 1969.

Marsden, E. W. *Technical Treatises*. Oxford, 1971.

Oldenstein, J. 'Zur Ausrüstung römischer Auxiliareinheiten', *Bericht der römisch-germanischen Kommission*, 57, 1976 (1977), 49-366.

Robinson, H. R. *The Armour of Imperial Rome*. Arms and Armour Press, 1975.

Rostovtzeff, M. I. (editor). *The Excavations at Dura-Europos*, sixth season. Yale University Press, 1936.

Schulten, A. *Numantia*, volumes 3 and 4. Bruckmann, 1927 and 1929.

Thomas, E. *Helme, Schilde, Dolche*. Akadémiai Kiadó, 1971.

Ulbert, G. *Römische Waffen des 1. Jahrhunderts n. Chr.* Limesmuseum Aalen, 1968.

Ulbert, G. 'Gladii aus Pompeji', *Germania*, 47 (1969), 97-128.

Ulbert, G. 'Straubing und Nydam. Zu römischen Langschwerten der späten Limeszeit' in G. Kossack and G. Ulbert (editors), *Studien zur vor- und frühgeschichtlichen Archäologie*. Beck, 1974, 197-216.

Ulbert, G. *Cáceres el Viejo*. Von Zabern, 1984.

Details of reconstruction work by the Ermine Street Guard can be found in their bulletin, *Exercitus*, from Oakland Farm, Dog Lane, Witcombe, Gloucestershire.

Index

Page numbers in italic refer to illustrations

Roman Military Equipment